W9-ANQ-560

Classical Music

Published by Smart Apple Media

1980 Lookout Drive, North Mankato, Minnesota 56003

Design and Production by EvansDay Design

Photographs: page 4: Dennis Marsico/CORBIS; pages 7, 18,
22, 25: Bettmann/CORBIS; pages 10, 11, 13, 14, 15, 17:
Archivo Iconografico, S.A./CORBIS; page 19: CORBIS;
page 21: Robbie Jack/CORBIS; page 23: Michael Nicholson/
CORBIS; page 27: Hulton-Deutsch Collection/CORBIS;
page 31: NealPreston/CORBIS

Library of Congress Cataloging-in-Publication Data

Kirgiss, Crystal.

Classical music / by Crystal Kirgiss

p. cm. — (World of music)

Includes index.

Summary: Surveys the history of Western classical music

from the Romantic symphonies to atonal music.

ISBN 1-58340-019-2

1. Classical music—History and criticism—Juvenile literature.

[1. Music—History and criticism.] I. Title.

II. Series: World of music (North Mankato, Minn.)

ML3928.G57   2002

781.6'8—dc21   98-042728

First Edition

2 4 6 8 9 7 5 3 1

09/02

WORLD OF MUSIC

Classical Music

CRYSTAL KIRGISS

IT IS MAY 7, 1824. IN A CONCERT HALL IN VIENNA, a conductor steps before a large choir and an orchestra of almost 100 people. His face filled with emotion, he leads them through a symphony of his own creation. Passion, rage, gentleness—all are reflected in each note being played, each word being sung. The music rises and falls. Then, all is silent. The end. The audience leaps to its feet, but the conductor stands motionless. A choir member gently turns him to face the audience: waving hats, clapping hands, and weeping. The conductor is Ludwig van Beethoven, who, by this time in his life, has become completely deaf. Even more remarkable is that nearly 200 years later, Beethoven's music still brings audiences to their feet and still moves many people to tears.

The 19th-century composer Hector Berlioz was not a great musician, but he was very creative. In his Symphonie Fantastique, *he had the string players tap the wooden side of their bows on the strings to create the sound of dancing skeletons.*

CLASSICAL MUSIC REALLY BEGAN WITH the Baroque era (the years 1600-1750). The word "baroque" refers to not only music but also art, architecture, and literature. During the Baroque era, more complex music evolved from the simple songs of the previous years. Singers and instrumentalists began adding ornamentation (extra notes) to dress up or decorate the music.

Johann Sebastian Bach, arguably the greatest musician of all time, lived during the Baroque era. As with most other musicians of his day, he was employed by several churches and royal courts. It was his job to write all of the music for Sunday worship. In his lifetime, he composed hundreds of pieces for chorus, organ, and orchestra.

Before the Baroque era, most music was written for human voices. Listeners loved the beautiful sounds produced by singers. Even well into the Baroque era, Italy—the center of all musical activity at that time—was in love with the opera. Instruments were considered dull in comparison to the human voice and

JOHANN SEBASTIAN BACH

were used mostly as background music for the singers.

At the height of opera's popularity, however, a young Italian named Antonio Stradivari changed the design of stringed instruments. With the changes, stringed instruments could produce tones as sweet and beautiful as those of a voice. The music produced by Stradivarius violins soon rivaled that of opera singers, and the symphony orchestra, as we know it today, was born.

VIOLIN, A POPULAR CLASSICAL INSTRUMENT

In 1862, composer Anton Rubinstein founded the first music conservatory in Russia. Peter Tchaikovsky, composer of the ballets Swan Lake, Sleeping Beauty, *and* The Nutcracker, *was one of its first graduates.*

THE MOST WIDELY KNOWN MEDIUM FOR classical music is a group of instruments collectively called the symphony orchestra. It consists of a string section (harp, violin, viola, cello, string bass); a woodwind section (flute, piccolo, oboe, English horn, clarinet, bass clarinet, bassoon, double bassoon); a brass section (French horn, trumpet, trombone, tuba); and a percussion section (timpani, tenor and bass drums, glockenspiel, chimes, celesta, cymbals, xylophone, and other rhythm instruments). In addition, there may be an organ, piano, saxophone, and other special instruments.

Around 1700, orchestras consisted of flutes, oboes, horns, and violins. Trumpets and timpani, or kettledrums, were sometimes added. In the mid-1700s, stringed instruments became the foundation of the orchestra. By the 1830s, the keys and valves on woodwind and brass instruments had been improved.

Hector Berlioz took advantage of those changes and began writing music that made

Frederick Chopin's Black Key Etude *was the first piano piece to play black notes with the thumb. It is featured in the Nancy Drew mystery volume 28,* The Clue of the Black Keys.

the most of each individual instrument's sound and tone. Orchestras of his era generally had about 100 members. This number became smaller in the early 1900s, and by the late 20th century, orchestras of all sizes could be heard, depending on what music was being performed.

COMPOSER JOHANN
STRAUSS II

THE CLASSICAL
Era

Domenico Scarlatti composed the Cat's Fugue *after his cat jumped up on his harpsichord while he was playing. Frederick Chopin composed the* Cat's Waltz *after his cat jumped up on his piano while he was composing.*

THE MID-18TH CENTURY USHERED IN the Classical era of music. Like their Baroque predecessors, Classical musicians often worked for a church, king, or nobleman. Then, in the late 18th century, Johann Christian Bach, the youngest son of Johann Sebastian, opened one of the first public concert halls in London. By 1800, most major European cities had their own. What had once been reserved for courts and royalty was at last made available to the general public.

As classical music became better known, people began buying sheet music to play in their own homes. Almost every upper-class household had a piano. After dinner, the

12

<small>YOUNG WOLFGANG
AMADEUS MOZART</small>

family would usually move to the music room and have an impromptu concert of piano solos or chamber music.

During this time, Wolfgang Amadeus Mozart was busy composing and performing the earliest of his nearly 700 symphonies, operas, concertos, sonatas, and other works. Mozart began performing publicly and composing at the age of four. Though he is now recognized as one of the greatest composers of all time, when he died at the age of 35, he was penniless and was buried in an unmarked grave.

Für Elise, *one of the world's most popular and well-known piano pieces, was really called* Für Therese *and was written by Beethoven for a girl he loved.*

Another Classical era musician, Franz Joseph Haydn, noticed that many audience members fell asleep during the slow movements of his symphonies. A fun-loving jokester, he wrote what is now known as "The Surprise Symphony." Just when he thought listeners might begin to nod off, he threw in a very loud and sudden bang from the entire orchestra.

Franz Joseph Haydn

During the Baroque era, Count Hermann Karl von Kayserling, the Russian ambassador to the Court of Dresden, hired full-time musicians to play for him at night whenever he couldn't fall asleep. They stayed in the next room and had to be ready to wake up at a moment's notice.

THE CLASSICAL ERA WAS FOLLOWED BY the Romantic era. This era featured the music of Ludwig van Beethoven, who had written his first three piano sonatas by the age of 13. Musicians, as well as artists and writers of the Romantic era, were obsessed with giving their creations meaning. They wanted their compositions to remind people of things, to heighten their emotions, and to move them to tears of joy or sorrow.

Frederick Chopin would cause the ladies to swoon when he played piano. Franz Liszt would fling his long hair while performing or conducting. Niccolo Paganini was con-

vinced that he wrote his violin concertos with help from the devil. Beethoven was known to rant and rave in angry outbursts, and then just as suddenly turn kind and gentle. Romanticists did not try to hide their emotions in either their private lives or their music. In their minds, the more love, sorrow, and happiness a person displayed, the better.

In his quest to compose meaningful and emotion-filled music, Richard Wagner forever changed the course of music history. He used the sounds of the orchestra to express

ARTIST'S RENDITION OF RICHARD WAGNER'S WILD MUSIC

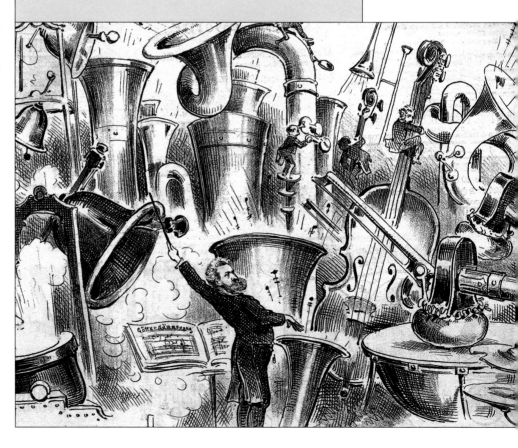

emotions that most people wanted to hide—anger, aggression, and eroticism. He wanted his music to be an emotional and psychological experience for the listener. People either loved it or hated it. He effectively divided the music public into those who preferred traditional music and those who were ready for new and contemporary sounds.

Italian composer and violinist Antonio Vivaldi wrote 94 operas; Mozart, from Austria, wrote his first opera at the age of 12; and German Johannes Brahms wrote numerous musical pieces in every form except the opera.

INTO THE
20th Century

Aleksandr Borodin was a 19th-century Russian composer who was also a chemistry professor in St. Petersburg. As a hobby, he studied music with two other famous composers, Franz Liszt and Nikolai Rimsky-Korsakov.

As the romantic era dissolved into the 20th Century era, musicians were divided into two main camps. There were the conservatives, who continued composing in traditional and familiar styles; and there were the progressives, who were determined to forge ahead and experiment with new sounds and styles.

Igor Stravinsky, like Richard Wagner before him, greatly influenced the music scene with his strange and disturbing music. His ballet, *The Rite of Spring*, is a perfect example. It is full of changing rhythms, shattering chords, unexpected outbursts of sound,

Scene from *The Rite of Spring*

ORCHESTRA
PERFORMING THE
FANTASIA
SOUNDTRACK

brutal and savage sound effects from percussion instruments, and phrases that re-
peat over and over again hypnotically.

The music depicts a ritual of pagan Russia, during which one of the ballerina
characters dances herself to death. When
the piece premiered in Paris in 1913, the
audience broke into a violent riot. This
piece of music, so hated at first, was later
featured in the Walt Disney film *Fantasia*'s
prehistoric sequence and received a full 15
minutes of applause when performed in
London in 1963.

Felix Mendelssohn wrote 12 symphonies, as well as the now-famous overture to Shakespeare's A Midsummer Night's Dream, *by the age of 17. He played piano for Queen Victoria of England and became her favorite composer.*

By the mid-1900s, technology had begun affecting music. With the availability of recordings, people around the world were able to hear a new composition almost immediately. The early eras of classical music each lasted between 100 and 150 years, but change happened much more quickly in the 20th century.

FELIX MENDELSSOHN

Franz Schubert of Vienna is considered by many historians to be the world's greatest songwriter. He composed 634 songs, called lieder, from the age of 18 until his death at age 31.

MANY CLASSICAL PIECES HAVE BEEN SO well-loved that they have been recorded many times by many different artists, rather than just one time like most popular songs. Some are so full of energy and variety that they have been widely used as background music for cartoons, movies, and commercials.

"The Sorcerer's Apprentice" by Frenchman Paul Dukas was made famous by Mickey Mouse in *Fantasia,* and "The William Tell Overture" was used as the theme for television's *The Lone Ranger.* Aaron Copland composed several film scores, including that of the James Dean film *Giant,* and his music was

used in the opening ceremonies of the 1984 Los Angeles Summer Olympics.

As more people were exposed to classical music in their everyday lives, they began to discover the musical genre's broad spectrum of instrument combinations and forms. Classical music could be sacred or secular, vocal or instrumental, bombastic or soothing, emotion-filled or nonsensical. It has always been up to the composer to decide which audience he or she wishes to reach.

UNIQUE
Sounds

*Franz Liszt invented a musical form
called the symphonic poem, which is
music that follows a piece of literature
such as a poem or a play. This form is
also sometimes called program music.*

LIKE LITERATURE AND ART, MUSIC IS AN
arena that allows people to express themselves
in new and unique ways. A particularly avant-
garde composer was John Cage. One of his
works, titled *4'3"*, was written for any group
of people and any group of instruments. The
composition requires them to simply sit on
the stage in silence. The sounds made by the
audience, the shifting of the performers, or
the outside traffic creates the music.

Composer George Crumb won the Pulit-
zer Prize in music in 1968 for *Echoes of Time
and the River,* which included, among various
strange instruments, a set of tuned water

26

JOHN CAGE (LEFT)

glasses. European composers Karlheinz Stockhausen and Pierre Boulez experimented with a technique called *musique concrete,* in which sounds from nature are recorded and then altered electronically in various ways.

In addition to experimentation, classical music began to embrace a wide variety of

ASIAN GONG
AND MALLET

world cultures. African tribal drums and Middle Eastern chanting were blended into composer Steve Reich's pieces. Many critics believe that Philip Glass, born in 1937, was the leading avant-garde musician of his time. He combined musical traditions from the East and West to create unique instrumental pieces and operas.

Composing took another sharp turn with the development of computers that made it possible to reproduce not only sound effects, but the sounds of an entire symphony orchestra without anyone actually playing. Small electronic keyboards made the art of composing music more accessible to students and music hobbyists. Virtually anyone with a desire to study and write music could create his or her own style.

Richard Wagner spent nine years creating The Ring of the Nibelung, *his cycle of four operas. To watch a production of the complete cycle, consisting of* Siegfried, The Valkyrie, The Rhinegold, *and* Gotterdammerung, *would take 16 hours.*

Six of the finest concertos in the world were written by Johann Sebastian Bach for Prince Margrave of Brandenburg, yet, at the prince's death, the music was considered to be worth only the equivalent of $4.50 in today's money.

PEOPLE HAVE DIFFERENT PERCEPTIONS of classical music. Some consider it boring and dull, others think it is only for the highbrow and serious, and still others think that anything classical is unpopular. But classical music is among the world's richest and most influential sources of entertainment.

Though not all people enjoy classical music, almost all of today's popular forms of music have classical roots. In fact, many contemporary recording artists, from the Beatles to Billy Joel and Elton John, have used classical music as a basis for their songs. No

BILLY JOEL ONSTAGE

matter what kind of music a person likes, there is probably some kind of classical music that he or she will like just as well. As one music expert said, "If people say they don't like classical music, it's only because they haven't found the right kind yet."